SAVINGS MIX

Savings Mix

How to Manage Money and Create Strategies to Achieve Savings and Goals

Sheila Atienza

Privilege Digital Media

Savings Mix: How to Manage Money and Create Strategies to
Achieve Savings and Goals

Savings Mix
Privilege Digital Media
Richmond, British Columbia
Canada

HARDCOVER ISBN: 978-1-990408-09-0

PAPERBACK ISBN: 978-0-9811475-5-0

EBOOK ISBN: 978-0-9811475-6-7

SUBJECT CATEGORIES:

BUSINESS. ECONOMICS.
Personal Finance. General.
Personal Finance. Money Management.
Personal Finance. Budgeting.
Personal Finance. Investing.

CONTENTS

DEDICATION

Dedicated to those
who strive to achieve financial independence

A QUICK NOTE FROM THE AUTHOR

"Sometimes, it does not matter how much possession you have in this world, but how that possession can inspire and motivate you to grow and make a difference in your life and others. That's what matters."

INTRODUCTION

Saving money is a creative process. So, where do you begin? How do you make money work for you? Are you curious or conscious of how your values can shape your ability to plan, save, spend and invest? How do you take charge, apply strategies and take actions?

In this book, **Savings Mix: How to Manage Money and Create Strategies to Achieve Savings and Goals,** we explore the money management fundamentals necessary to build and achieve a healthy personal financial lifestyle. This book can best be used as a beginner's guide to personal finance. You will learn the art of managing and saving money; and how the process can practically work for you.

This book has seven chapters. Chapter One introduces us to the world of personal finance. Chapter Two explores money, credit, and debt. Chapter Three discusses money management. Chapter Four explores topics in creating a strategic approach. Chapter Five discusses achieving savings and goals. Chapter Six and Chapter Seven, respectively, explore creating a healthy savings mix and investment mix.

In **Chapter One, Personal Finance, Lifestyle, and Basic Decisions: An Overview,** we touch on:

- The World That We Live In
- What Does Being Wealthy Mean to You?
- Personal Finance: Understanding and Analyzing Your Personal Financial Choices, Decisions and Actions
- Personal Finance: Taking Charge, Planning, and Taking Actions

In **Chapter Two, Money, Credit, and Debt,** we cover the following:

- What Money Means to People
- What is Debt and Why We Accumulate Debts?
- Are All Debts Bad?
- Borrowing and Spending
- Debt, Debtor, Creditor
- Why People Borrow Money
- More Expenses, More Borrowing
- What is Credit and Do We Need It?
- Understanding Your Credit Worthiness
- Credit Rating, Credit Report
- Should You Apply for Credit?
- Working On Your Credit Rating
- How to Improve Credit Rating
- How Do You Know If You Are in Debt Trouble?

In **Chapter Three, Why Money Management is Essential,** we cover the following:

- What is Personal Money Management?
- Why Personal Money Management is Essential
- Understanding and Using Financial Resources
- Knowing that You Can Control Your Finances
- Achieving a Sense of Financial Independence
- Achieving Better Relationships and Other Personal Rewards
- Needs versus Wants
- What Are Your Financial Priorities?

In **Chapter Four, Planning and Managing Money: Creating A Strategic Approach,** we cover the following:

- PHASE 1: Where are you at this point? Understand your personal financial position
- PHASE 2: What are your financial needs and goals: Know how you can accomplish your goals
- PHASE 3: What financial strategies or options do you have?
- PHASE 4: Assess your options. Are these feasible?
- PHASE 5: Develop, Write and Execute Your Financial Action Plan
- PHASE 6: Evaluate, Adjust and Rework Your Action Plan

In **Chapter Five, Achieving Savings Goals,** we cover the following:

- Personal Thoughts about Money
- Determining your Money Habits and Lifestyle
- Embracing Change, New Habits and Skills
- Challenges with Saving Money
- Finding Answers to Important Questions about Saving Money
- How Will You Save Money
- Saving Money is a Creative Process
- Pay Yourself First
- Your Financial Goal and Savings Plan
- When Will You Begin Saving?
- Decide Where to Save Money
- Making Money Work for You
- Have You Heard About the Rule of 72?
- Saving Money versus Investing Money
- How Values Shape Your Planning to Save and Spend

In **Chapter Six, Creating a Healthy Savings Mix,** we cover the following topics:

- Creating a Healthy Savings Mix: What Are You Saving For?
- Creating a Healthy Savings Mix: Making Your SMART Goal
- How Do You Know You Are Achieving Your Goal?
- Can You Attain Your Goals?
- Self-Image, Confidence and Opportunities
- Do You Find Your Goal Reasonable, Relevant and Realistic?

- Does Your Goal Have a Deadline?
- What Are You Saving For?

And finally, in **Chapter Seven, Creating Your Investment Mix as a Beginning Investor,** we cover the following topics:

- Where to Put Your Money
- A Whole New Journey
- Savings Account
- Investment Mix and Diversification
- Should You Do Stock Investing
- Mutual Funds
- Exchange Traded Funds
- Robo-advisor
- Conclusion

ONE

PERSONAL FINANCE, LIFESTYLE, AND BASIC DECISIONS

Personal Finance, Lifestyle,
and Basic Decisions
An Overview

CHAPTER ONE

- The World That We Live In
- What Does Being Wealthy Mean to You?
- Personal Finance: Understanding and Analyzing Your Personal Financial Choices, Decisions and Actions
- Personal Finance: Taking Charge, Planning, and Taking Actions

THE WORLD THAT WE LIVE IN

We are living in a world in which we face uncertainty. We know that a global crisis and national economic challenges are likely to happen whether we like it or not. And as such, it would lead people to make personal financial decisions.

It is alarming, though, to know that more and more people make poor day-to-day decisions based on the available choices. And that could lead to some possible adverse actions.

In the process, many people could end up with more problems, experiencing unfortunate circumstances.

You probably have heard about a growing number of people and companies declaring bankruptcies, if not, resorting to credit counselling or making financial arrangements with banks and lenders.

It is not uncommon that we hear some people approaching house foreclosure proceedings. Some people, meanwhile, cannot seem to be approved of a financing loan. Others are in a hand-to-mouth situation and even facing difficulties paying bills and apartment rent.

Some people are doing just fine. Probably, their concerns are simply about not having enough savings in the bank or even in other forms of investments. They could not seem to set aside some funds to use for house purchase down payment, car, or education.

Despite earning a regular monthly income, sometimes, you feel that finding and saving extra money for the future would seem impossible.

How does one proceed from here?

If you want to achieve and maintain sound financial wellness, you will have to develop your ability to make vital decisions in managing your money.

And that is knowing when, why, and how you control the use of money - your very own money - your hard-earned MONEY.

WHAT DOES BEING WEALTHY MEAN TO YOU?

Of course, the term 'wealth' is subjective and may connote different meanings to each of us.

You may define wealth as having many assets and properties, such as real estate investments, stocks, cars, and other luxurious items. Or you may associate it as being satisfied enough, having not to experience some anxieties, especially when paying bills and other fees.

Others look at the term 'wealthy' as being able to retire from a nine-to-five job. Or they could look at it as being able to sustain self-employment.

Some people, however, would associate the term 'wealthy' as having enough money to afford retirement. Or to pursue other interests.

How people perceive money would depend on their ultimate goals and satisfaction in life. That would reflect the kind of lifestyle they want and how they feel and think about it.

In most cases, how people become wealthy would depend on how they manage money, spend money and save money.

People may pursue a profitable small business or good-paying jobs, but if they do not know how to manage money wisely, they may experience financial challenges along the way.

People make choices. People define their lifestyle. The question, therefore, that we should ask is: "Am I comfortable with my current lifestyle?" If not, then, "What kind of lifestyle would I rather have?"

If you are asked the hypothetical, popular question, "What would you do if, all of a sudden, you won in a contest or lottery some millions of dollars?" How would you respond to various scenarios?

Where would you spend the money?

How would you spend it?

How long do you think the money would last?

Would you quit your job?

Would you start a business?

Would you go for travel?

Would you go for education?

Would you ask a personal financial consultant to help you plan your future?

Of course, the odds of winning some millions of dollars may seem slim, but not impossible.

We know that it does not happen to all people. But the possibility of receiving a huge sum of money may occur at some point in our life.

What if you get a salary raise or a bonus? Or if you own a small business, and surprisingly you land a huge account or most sought-after client, which may lead to large billings, would you know what to do? Would you be prepared to handle such a rare opportunity?

Do you have a plan, just in case?

It is important to note that receiving more money or having more dollars in one's pocket would not necessarily create a successful financial outcome.

Just imagine how many stories we could hear about one-day millionaires, casino players, instant contest winners, or lottery winners ending up miserably.

Did you know that many end up with more money problems and debts?

Some would overspend their winnings, while others would abuse and misuse the funds.

The way people lead their day-to-day activities would contribute to their financial future. And the way they adhere to certain beliefs and manifest their values would, likewise, reflect on their disposition that would have an impact on their lifestyle.

Sometimes, it does not matter how much possession you have in this world, but how that possession can inspire and motivate you to grow and make a difference in your life and others. That's what matters.

Sometimes, it does not matter
how much possession you have in this world
but how that possession can inspire and
motivate you to grow
and make a difference
in your life and others.
That's what matters.

***

Now, let us look at another scenario.

What if you are offered by your bank a credit account with a credit limit that would allow up to ten thousand (10,000) dollars, would you accept it?

What for would you use the credit?

Would you max out the limit?

When would you plan to pay it back?

How would you be able to settle the amount that you borrowed (which at that point becomes a form of debt)?

Could the debt payment be covered through your gross monthly income?

Life is full of unexpected scenarios. The ability to make smart decisions would therefore be of paramount importance. People must be forewarned and be prepared to handle different financial circumstances. Situations involving money and personal decisions come with many challenges.

Making money is one thing. Managing money is another. And the truth is - it is not that easy to work on money matters.

But we could always learn.

And the point alone of wanting to learn after a misstep - is a beginning of looking after your well-being.

Smart money management is hard work. It requires focus, commitment, and discipline.

Know what matters. Know how managing money works and how it can help you in your overall approach with your finances.

Smart money management is hard work. It requires focus, commitment, and discipline.

***

PERSONAL FINANCE:
UNDERSTANDING AND ANALYZING
YOUR PERSONAL FINANCIAL CHOICES,
DECISIONS AND ACTIONS

Each day, we may face different situations. Some of these situations may seem familiar to us, while some may put us in an awkward position, especially if we are to make decisions. Some may lead us to go through a life awakening experience.

Problems involving money may result in debt challenges that can trigger even more. Until we could feel so overwhelmed and therefore we could not manage anymore.

We can experience stress and discomfort, tiredness, sleepless nights, and relationship conflicts.

What most of us do not realize in the process is that we create our actions based on our choices and decisions.

Now, consider the following questions and analyze your responses and the decisions you are going to make.

When faced with making a big, bold financial decision, do you seek help through various sources, such as consulting others for opinions, talking to a professional, or finding other information online?

Do you have specific financial goals for the short-term period and long-term period? If so, would you write down your goals and plans?

Can you rationalize your goals?

Why do you want to achieve a specific goal?

Do you find your goals achievable in the next year or so?

Are you aware of any risks involved with your financial choices and decisions?

Do you have any personal guidelines and rules for budgeting, saving, and spending?

Whenever we experience a challenging financial situation that would require financial decisions, we must learn to pause awhile. We must take the time to think and then prepare some plans. The objective here is to look at the situation carefully. Think through all possible angles of the problem. What are the possible risks for each step of the action that you will do? Would it add more harm to the issue? Or would the risk be worth it in the long run?

Planning is like creating a map or flowchart that helps you understand what could probably be the scenario if you take upon a particular step.

That would enable you to prepare to handle each of the possible scenarios.

Of course, you could not always predict the outcome of each of the steps. But, at least you've given yourself some warnings, and you can, in one way or another, deal with the challenges.

Remember, if and when you worry about money matters, the most important thing to avoid (as early as possible) is to get into a much deeper problem.

That would include not just the financial aspects but the legal aspects as well.

**

PERSONAL FINANCE: TAKING CHARGE, PLANNING, AND TAKING ACTIONS

At this point in your life, would you say that you feel you are in charge, and consequently, accountable for your actions? How do you go about planning and doing your day-to-day finances? How do you set your rules or guidelines for yourself to take action?

When people are able to manage their money and work on their finances, they tend to feel a different level of fulfillment. They find a good sense of confidence in themselves. They feel already successful by merely managing a considerable amount of dollars each day.

Some people find that being able to settle debts (and oversee financial obligations) while at the same time still being able to save some amount of money could already call it an achievement in itself. After all, everyone is not able to do and accomplish such a goal.

Money management is a personal matter.

Money management is a personal matter.

Every person has different financial goals. And so is the level of satisfaction one hopes to achieve.

People must understand and spell out their financial priorities. That would mean identifying the most basic needs. That would mean putting much attention to the things that you require for some comfort and survival.

TWO

MONEY, CREDIT, AND DEBT

Money, Credit, and Debt

CHAPTER TWO

- What Money Means to People
- What is Debt and Why We Accumulate Debts?
- Are All Debts Bad?
- Borrowing and Spending
- Debt, Debtor, Creditor
- Why People Borrow Money
- More Expenses, More Borrowing
- What is Credit and Do We Need It?
- Understanding Your Credit Worthiness
- Credit Rating, Credit Report
- Should You Apply for Credit?
- Working On Your Credit Rating
- How to Improve Credit Rating
- How Do You Know If You Are in Debt Trouble?

WHAT MONEY MEANS TO PEOPLE

We always associate the word money with spending or purchasing products and services. After a day's work, we expect to earn some form of income. Then, we spend money for something – and many more things.

That is how simple it is to understand money, right?

Actually, people know the answer to this. However, people don't always recognize the signs. If only we can say how simple money works, then the world of personal finance would be easy to deal with.

The truth is, money is not just about spending or buying.

Money shapes our way of living.

In fact, some people regard money the way they achieve things. Sometimes, people feel that they fail if they do not make enough money – or if they could not afford to live a lavish lifestyle.

Money tends to create an impact on how people view themselves - and how they think others view their status in life. Some people tend to join certain groups – the big spenders or the high rollers. They do such things sometimes just to keep up with the 'Joneses'. The sad reality is - they may follow the trend beyond what they can afford.

People tend to forget money is not everything. It is only a resource and tool to meet our financial goals. People must recognize how to take control of this powerful tool.

When we know how to exercise control, we have a greater chance to create a wonderful world of finance for ourselves.

Now, what happens when people go out of control and cannot manage their money?

This can result in POOR SPENDING, which eventually could lead to unwanted DEBTS – and more unwanted debts.

WHAT IS DEBT AND WHY WE ACCUMULATE DEBTS?

Debt is a popular word that seems to dwell with us from the moment we become part of this credit economy.

Everywhere we go there are always things that would trigger our emotion to act on spending.

From the time we think about pursuing a college program and applying for student loans, to finding and using our access to more loans, such as credit cards or lines of credit, car loans, and mortgage loans, we find ourselves overwhelmed with a number of debts to settle.

And there are people who seem to be more accustomed to the idea of taking on more debts and loans.

Many consumers have become even more familiar with other forms of debt.

Perennial shoppers are hopping from one department store to another. They would use their store charge cards and would do shopping even more often. Consumers see product offerings and feel tempted to take advantage of irresistible promotional offers.

It is so much easier to get into loads of debt, especially when a person has access to borrowing.

But is it also easy to get out of debt?

While no one could absolutely tell the answer to this question - since this topic about debt is a personal matter, only the person who gets into such a debt situation can decide on how to go about it.

Although, in most cases, it is not easy, it still would depend on the person who opted to borrow and carry debts.

ARE ALL DEBTS BAD?

There are two ways we look at debts.

There are debts that are classified as bad. And there are debts that are viewed as good.

Let us explore further.

If we purchase items using a credit card, the obligation is to pay back the borrowed amount.

If we could not pay back the entire borrowed amount, there could be even more challenges to go through when settling the debt.

The credit card balance that is carried over the next month and following months, and more months, could lead to more charges. These charges may include higher interest rates, penalties, and fees. You may end up not aware of how much you owe. You may even be surprised with the outstanding balance due.

These are debts that are accumulated as consumer debt, such as when we buy a pair of shoes, electronic gadgets, computers, furniture, vehicles, appliances, and other consumer products that could lose monetary value over time.

These debts only add up (as liability) and do not increase in value (or do not become an asset or equity).

Now there are debts that may qualify as good debt.

Getting a mortgage loan to help finance a home purchase can be a good thing. We know that with real estate, an owner can build equity on the property over time, which can then become an asset.

There's a big caution here, though.

You have to make sure that you can afford mortgage payments and other housing costs that are associated with owning a home before deciding to get a mortgage.

Ensure that you have access to your emergency funds. That could cover mortgage payments in case you lose your job and other financial resources.

Some people lose their property and equity in the form of foreclosure when they could not meet their mortgage obligations.

BORROWING AND SPENDING

Many people think about the idea of borrowing money at some point in their lives.

After all, many homeowners have purchased their homes through home mortgage financing. Without the help of a lender, they would not be able to achieve their goals of owning a home.

As you can see, borrowing money in the form of credit is not always a bad thing.

You have to examine carefully whether taking on debts would make sense.

What is important is to understand how to manage finances effectively, which should include managing debt repayments, and prioritizing needs and goals.

Borrowing money to spend on things you do not need and you cannot afford could be disastrous and could lead to financial problems.

Some people could get in trouble when they are not able to take control of their credit.

DEBT, DEBTOR, CREDITOR

Let us explore a few more things about borrowing.

You probably have heard of the financial terms, debt, debtor, and creditor.

You become a debtor when you borrow money from another person or entity (who then becomes your creditor).

Your debt is the money that you owe, or simply put your liability.

WHY PEOPLE BORROW MONEY

Borrowing has become more like a trend today. People tend to borrow more money these days than many years ago.

One of the reasons could be that people see more income opportunities and earn higher incomes today than many decades ago.

Because of this, many people think that they have more power in their hands to access borrowed money.

Also, at the increasing rate of market prices today, people can't help but think of borrowing.

And since lenders could offer a much lower interest rate, many people are attracted by the availability of a low-cost borrowing rate.

Then, if we would look at the scenario of what is happening today, we could observe that many people spend money more than they earn. They borrow money to cover expenses they could not handle from their income.

MORE EXPENSES, MORE BORROWING

There are many other reasons why people borrow more money.

Unexpected expenditures and emergency cases do come up.

Then, there are cases in which people could not resist purchasing certain big-ticketed items.

And there are opportunities that would require some money, not to mention looking at investment possibilities and venturing into entrepreneurship. And how about paying for huge travel expenses? Then, of course, there are educational courses and programs that would require a substantial amount of money to pay for tuition fees and other charges.

Therefore, borrowing has become part of today's financial lifestyle.

People use different types of borrowing depending on their purpose and need.

Most people these days recognize the use of credit cards. Also, many retail stores offer store charge cards to their customers and frequent shoppers. The idea is that - the more customers buy, the better it would be for both the consumers and the retailers. Some credit card companies could offer rewards to card users as part of their loyalty marketing. The more frequent shoppers use the card, the more points they could earn. And that could also lead to getting free items as part of customer's rewards.

Other people agree to installment financing, while there are some people who would apply for consumer loans. Those who are starting their small business would apply for some types of business loans. And, of course, those who need to purchase a home might need a mortgage.

Indeed, financial activities such as spending, borrowing, and using credit have become part of human reality. And it will continue to affect how people live and how one will get on in the future.

People must pay attention to their credit and debt situations and ensure that their act of borrowing will not damage their well-being.

Unfortunately, for some people, debts have almost ruined their life. The level of financial burdens particularly, consumer debts, have increased dramatically. Millions of consumers experience overwhelming personal debts. And they could not seem to get out of it.

WHAT IS CREDIT AND DO WE NEED IT?

Despite the growing number of people getting into financial trouble, the reality remains, we live in a world where credit gets the global economy going.

We may not like it, but people need to borrow money in the form of credit or loan at some point. This act of borrowing money could result in debt accumulation.

Before people could borrow money to fulfill their needs, they need to prove to creditors that they are trustworthy to use and manage their credit.

Before people could borrow money to fulfill their needs, they need to prove to creditors that they are trustworthy to use and manage their credit.

When people purchase items, such as a car, and various highly-priced ticketed items, and even real estate, they must be qualified and get approved for financing.

Also, some service companies, such as cable, hydro, and telecommunication companies and even some landlords and prospective employers, may require some background checks.

A credit report is one of the essential requirements before borrowers can get approved for financing.

Hence, lenders and creditors look at the borrowers' credit profile to determine their credit-worthiness.

UNDERSTANDING YOUR CREDIT WORTHINESS

Have you ever wondered why some people seem to be good candidates to pursue credit applications? Yet, other people seem to struggle with these financing and credit aspects.

Well, as mentioned earlier, borrowers are assessed according to their credit-worthiness.

There are, at least, three essential factors that would contribute to achieving credit-worthiness.

And these factors would pertain to the borrower's capacity, responsibility, and assets.

The first factor refers to the capacity of the borrower to pay for the requested credit or loan.
Creditors would look at incomes and determine whether borrowers' incomes could service their debts. Lenders or banks would basically want to find out whether the borrower can afford making regular payments.

Also, the creditor would need to know if there are other expenses and debts a borrower needs to settle, and that would make it difficult for the borrower to make the required payments.

Next, the borrowers need to prove how responsible and dependable they are in keeping up with their agreement to pay back the loan.
At this point the creditor examines the character of the borrowers. They would need to know the nature of

the job and how stable the borrowers are in their current jobs.

Creditors would further assess how long borrowers have been working with their present employer. Or if they own their business, what is the nature of self-employment and whether income taxes are paid on time.

In addition, borrowers would need to disclose their residential address, how long they have lived in that address, as well as where they have lived in the past.

Just bear in mind, creditors have their criteria to determine trustworthiness.

The borrowers simply need to satisfy the lender or bank with the essential requirements and to prove that they are trustworthy.

And the one other factor that may also be necessary is your assets. That could refer to anything you own that has monetary value. Your assets list may include equity in your home, savings, securities or stocks, cars, and other personal properties.

Always remember that creditors need some kind of assurance or protection in case of default.

Borrowers' assets can help prove that in such a case, they can liquidate or sell assets, if and when the situation calls for it.

As a whole, it is imperative to say that a lender is interested in knowing what sort of properties borrowers own. What is the value of borrowers' assets and other properties (that can serve as financial collateral)? What financial burdens and debts do borrowers have? Are borrowers reliable? Could they commit to the agreement? How much do borrowers earn?

When a borrower gets approved for credit or loan, creditors assign a credit limit amount to the account, depending on the borrower's income and credit history.

CREDIT RATING, CREDIT REPORT

Many people may not be aware of credit rating. But, creditors, lenders, banks and other financial institutions use credit information about people who borrow money in the form of credit or loan.

The credit information reflects how good or bad the borrower is when it comes to paying back loans and other debts.

Are borrowers able to pay on time or are they always late in sending payments?

Have the borrowers filed for debt consolidation or bankruptcy?

Credit rating agencies (or credit reporting institutions) in Canada and the USA, such as the leading reporting agencies, Equifax and TransUnion, keep information and credit profile of borrowers.

Creditors would first check with the credit rating agencies the borrowers' credit scores before they could approve the loan.

By generating a credit report, lenders will have an idea about the credit-worthiness of the borrowers.

SHOULD YOU APPLY FOR CREDIT?

Do you have any plans of buying a home several months or years from now? Or do you have other financial goals - such as starting a new business, buying some equipment necessary to operate your small enterprise, and other important stuff - that would require some funds?

When do you think you would need the loan?

If you think credit is something that you find useful and believe you would need it at some point to accomplish your financial goal, you may start to consider the idea and learn thoroughly about the process.

One thing important to note about credit is that, sometimes, it may be even more challenging to obtain a loan at the time you need it as compared to when you do not need it.

Borrowers must prepare all the necessary requirements and work on improving their financial knowledge.

Some creditors and lenders look at some possible red flags. And if they find that borrowers are desperate to access funds, they would start to wonder. Lenders might even doubt and think twice about granting a loan.

WORKING ON YOUR CREDIT RATING

Even though borrowing money in the form of credit may not be something that you need at this point, you should start to think about the importance of building credit as early as possible.

Granting you never know when you would need it, but what if the time comes you realize you need to access it, right?

Life could be unpredictable. And there is a chance in the future that you may need more funds than you think you would, especially in case of an emergency. Would you not prepare as early as you can – and avoid being desperate looking to borrow some money when no one could extend monetary help?

Somehow, it is a smart move to have an option to borrow money. Even the richest people in the world know the importance of having the leverage and ability to borrow money.

Once you have access to credit, the very important thing you have to ensure is that you're able to work on improving your credit rating. Learn about obtaining credit reports by visiting the credit reporting agencies online. When you receive your personal credit report, you will know where you stand. You will find out about your credit score and review your credit history.

Working on your credit is not a one-time task. It is a continuous process, in which you will have to integrate within your day-to-day way of living. That will include: how you settle your bills and other financial obligations, how often you use your credit card with your purchases, and how you set aside some funds for future use.

HOW TO IMPROVE CREDIT RATING

One would think this is very basic and simple. But if it is, you would wonder, why do some people end up with poor credit scores and find it difficult to get approved for a loan or financing?

Here are some important points to consider.

Make sure that you are repaying debts on the required schedule. If possible, before the due date.

Try to borrow only the amount that you believe you can afford to pay back.

Set your own amount limit to borrowing even if your actual credit limit is higher than what you need. In other words, do not max out your credit. In this way, you know you are comfortable with managing payments and you stay with your financial comfort level.

Once you get approved for credit, do not apply for more credit.

Be forewarned that when you submit credit applications to more than one lender (or creditor) at the same time, and you do this frequently (say every few weeks), this can post warnings to creditors. Your credit rating will be affected negatively.

Read all the wordings and 'fine print' in your credit or loan agreement. And make sure that you understand what you are getting into before you sign on the dotted line.

Do not get overwhelmed with the length of the paperwork. Take the time to go over and read the entire document.

Also, be careful when someone asks you to co-sign a loan. Remember, when you do this, you also assume the responsibility of the other person. It can also affect your credit rating if and when the other person defaults.

If you are not comfortable with being a co-signer, you can decline politely and explain the consequences on your part.

Remember, when you cannot commit to your agreement, not only are you paying at a higher interest rate with penalties and other charges, you are also directly damaging your credit rating.

There are many more ways you could do in order to improve your credit rating.

Pay off your balance, if at all possible. If you do carry a balance, try to pay more than the minimum amount. Also, always avoid late payments.

Do not attempt to send more credit requests (to one lender, then another lender). If you are hoping to get approved for a much higher credit limit, you should, perhaps, wait for some more time. Wait for more than six months, if possible, before you try applying again. It is even better to skip the idea of applying for more credit. That is to avoid posing red flags. You do not want lenders to think that you are desperate.

Lastly, deal with reputable creditors only. After all, good creditors want to deal with trustworthy borrowers.

HOW DO YOU KNOW IF YOU ARE IN DEBT TROUBLE?

People incur debts for different reasons. It's only a matter of time before one could realize that getting out of a debt situation can be challenging (if not too complicated).

Imagine you are not only paying for the loan principal (or the amount that you have used or borrowed originally), but you are also paying for the interest and other fees (and charges). Now, if you do not pay off the entire balance, it will, then, be carried over the following month (or months). That means you could be paying more. You would be surprised to find out the owing amount could be substantial. If you pay the minimum amount only, it could take several years before you could complete your loan payments.

Some people could go through such a scenario. Then, they could get into more loads of debt, causing them to experience more financial problems.

Let us explore some signs that tell us when a person could be in debt danger:

- *Are you not able to set aside some money to meet your financial obligations?*
- *Are you finding it hard to save some money?*
- *Are you maxing out your credit limit on most of your credit accounts?*
- *Are you often short of funds?*
- *Are you missing payments for more than a month?*
- *Are you always paying only the minimum?*

- *Are you not confident that you can set a payment schedule to pay off the entire loan balance, say in 12 or 24 months?*
- *Are you paying a higher interest rate?*
- *Are you not aware of the total amount you owe from your creditors?*
- *Are you always seeking to borrow money from others?*
- *Are you finding it hard to sleep because of your debts?*

And there are other things people may experience when they have debt problems.

Can you think and clarify your thoughts about money, credit, and debt?

* * *

THREE

WHY MONEY MANAGEMENT IS ESSENTIAL

Why Money Management is Essential

CHAPTER THREE

- What is Personal Money Management?
- Why Personal Money Management is Essential
- Understanding and Using Financial Resources
- Knowing that You Can Control Your Finances
- Achieving a Sense of Financial Independence
- Achieving Better Relationships and Other Personal Rewards
- Needs versus Wants
- What Are Your Financial Priorities?

WHAT IS PERSONAL MONEY MANAGEMENT?

Personal money management is a creative, disciplined, methodical personal finance approach that results from establishing financial priorities, organizing financial resources, preparing schedules and planning a course of actions.

Personal money management is a creative, disciplined, methodical personal finance approach that results from establishing financial priorities, organizing financial resources, preparing schedules and planning a course of actions. Ultimately, with smart money management, people can accomplish a great sense of financial fulfillment.

When people are able to handle their day-to-day finances, they must be doing things that would contribute to their overall financial health. They must be in control of their financial activities, from spending to saving money. They must know what would make sense given their situation. They would take action based on their needs.

Coming up with a thorough personal financial plan can help achieve better decisions. Such decisions can lessen the 'unknowns' and help prepare better for the present and the future.

With utmost focus and commitment in managing money, people can look forward to a financial future that speaks for their values and beliefs.

WHY PERSONAL MONEY MANAGEMENT IS ESSENTIAL

So, let us take a look at the **reasons why money management is essential in our daily life:**

You will be able to understand, recognize and use financial resources more effectively.

You will feel confident as you learn to take control of your finances.

You will be able to achieve a sense of fulfillment and financial independence.

You will be able to achieve better relationships and other personal rewards.

UNDERSTANDING AND USING
FINANCIAL RESOURCES

Each person has different financial circumstances. When we think about managing money, it is a given that people have their respective financial resources.

Some people are gainfully employed. They are working full-time and earning regular good monthly income. Others have their small business or even doing some part-time jobs. Some may work freelance or on a contractual arrangement.

In the process, people accumulate wealth. When you receive your monthly pay, you now have the power to decide what to do with the money that you have earned.

You will allocate, perhaps, some of the funds for your bill payments. Some people would have their way of setting aside some funds with the objective of paying themselves through some form of savings. Such savings can either be put through the basic savings account or retirement savings account (like the RRSP or TFSA in Canada or the IRA/401K in the US); and even other open-investment accounts.

Sooner or later, people obtain access to borrowing or credit lines. They may use their approved credit, such as a credit card or unsecured line of credit. Also, many people with good credit scores tend to purchase a home. And therefore decide to carry a mortgage.

And of course, there are other financial resources people could use, depending on their financial situation.

Planning on how to use available financial resources would be fundamental in handling personal finances.

When a person effectively uses and manages the financial resources, one will likely see better results; and that can contribute to the person's overall financial health.

Can you think and identify what financial resources are available to you at this point?

* * *

KNOWING THAT YOU CAN CONTROL YOUR FINANCES

With money management, you would be able to develop your ability to look after your financial health and look to the direction you are heading.

You would be broad-minded. You would look at your financial decisions based on a sound assessment. You would be able to identify and review financial risks and outcomes that could come with your decisions.

In the process, you would know how vital it is to avoid unnecessary debt, personal loans, department store card charges, dependence on other people for financial assistance, debt consolidation, and bankruptcy.

ACHIEVING A SENSE OF FINANCIAL INDEPENDENCE

Personal money management would allow you to attain a sense of financial success and freedom by focusing not just on your needs but your financial goals as well.

You would be able to determine and project the necessary expenses.

You would know whether your expenses are valid as real needs and not just the nice-to-have or nice-to-do things. As such, you would know how to balance things out. You would know how to have fun while at the same time you are focused on working on your finances. You would be carrying out a series of activities that you must do to achieve your financial goals.

When you are good at managing your finances, you will feel proud of yourself. You would feel more confident. You would appreciate the kind of financial security that you have. You would enjoy your day-to-day life free from financial worries.

How amazing would that be, right?

ACHIEVING BETTER RELATIONSHIPS AND OTHER PERSONAL REWARDS

When your financial activities are in place, you will experience improved communication with the people around you, especially your family. You would also be able to understand others better.

You would be able to perform well at work and inspire others with your determination and hard work. Of course, all these would result from well-planned decisions and well-executed financial strategies.

* * *

NEEDS VERSUS WANTS

It is human nature for people to need and want something. However, sometimes people do not recognize how important it is to focus on things that qualify as really necessary.

When people go to the mall and see shops, they tend to look around and buy things according to impulse. It is as if people do not realize that merchants and retailers do their promotional campaigns to lure shoppers into their stores. Retailers have designed their marketing and promotional strategies so that people would get attracted to their offerings.

When you happen to be in a situation in which you are lured into buying something, you could end up accumulating things. Without realizing first whether you need it or not, you could hurt your financial position.

Spending money seems way easy. What is difficult is to be able to spend money smartly.

As such, it would be imperative to distinguish wants from needs. When you go through the process of organizing (and improving) your finances, it would be vital, first and foremost, to identify and focus on your needs as opposed to wants.

We qualify our spending as 'needs' according to whether these things are vital in order to survive with day-to-day living. Typically, needs are those things that people would consider as the essentials. Basic needs would include shelter, food, water, and clothing. These things are absolutely necessary to human existence.

There are also things that people need to factor in to ensure that basic needs are met. For example, when you go to work, you would need a form of transportation. Also, when looking at your well-being, you would need certain things so that you are capable of functioning well at work; and at home, doing household chores and other daily activities.

Needs can be those things you need to fulfill on a routine basis.

Before you decide to spend on something, you have to qualify whether these things are actually in the category of your needs.

People may be surprised to realize there are many things they buy that actually would not go into the category of 'needs' but would fall into the category of 'wants'.

'Wants' equate to things or ideas we want or wish to have but not really a necessity.

What people consider as nice-to-do and nice-to-have do not fundamentally reflect human survival.

Activities such as going out to buy things on impulse, dining out in fancy restaurants, and even subscribing to the latest technology craze, would not qualify as things you need for survival, but nice things to do or to have.

Your deliberation would depend on how these things serve your purpose. You may decide to look at these 'wants and wishes' perhaps after you have worked on your basic needs and priorities.

By now, you can start to see the difference. You will have to look at things according to your priorities.

WHAT ARE YOUR FINANCIAL PRIORITIES?

You will need to know and assess your financial priorities before you could accomplish your short-term and long-term goals.

What are your needs? Do you need to pay regular monthly rent or mortgage? How about arranging for your car payments, house insurance, apartment utilities, and internet subscription? Or do you need to start saving money for your emergency fund?

FOUR

PLANNING AND MANAGING MONEY: CREATING A STRATEGIC APPROACH

Planning and Managing Money:
Creating A Strategic Approach

CHAPTER FOUR

- **PHASE 1**: Where are you at this point? Understand your personal financial position
- **PHASE 2**: What are your financial needs and goals?
- **PHASE 3**: What financial strategies or options do you have?
- **PHASE 4**: Assess your options. Are these feasible?
- **PHASE 5**: Develop, write and execute your Financial Action Plan
- **PHASE 6**: Evaluate, adjust and rework your Action Plan

PLANNING AND MANAGING MONEY: CREATING A STRATEGIC APPROACH

PHASE 1: Where are you at this point?
Understand Your Personal Financial Position

The very first thing that you will need to do - when creating your strategic approach - is to understand and analyze your current personal financial position. You will need to look at your situation more closely - where are you at this point?

You can ask yourself the following questions.
What are your sources of income?
How much are you earning a month?
How much savings do you have?
Do you own any assets that have financial value?
How many adult members are in your immediate family circle?
How many family members are working and contributing to your household gross monthly income?

Next, you will need to list down all of your living expenses.
You may include: mortgage payments or rental payments, utilities, foods, supplies, car payments, transportation expenses, insurance, and other monthly fixed payments.

Now, you will also need to determine any debts that you carry.

This may include credit card payments, personal loans or line of credit.

Write down and prepare a record of your assets and liabilities.

Completing a list of your personal financial activities and obligations on a regular basis will help you get organized. This will also serve as your guide in doing your personal financial planning.

Can you think of your current financial situation, in terms of income, living expenses, debts, or any owing amounts, as well as savings or any other personal financial assets that you own at this point?

* * *

PHASE 2: What Are Your Financial Needs and Goals: Know how you can accomplish your goals

We all could agree that people have different needs and aspirations in life.

At this point, you will need to think of your personal financial goals.

Goals may be immediate or for the future. You may need to look at the bigger picture and see how these would come into your overall financial plan. You will need to classify these goals - whether you would like to accomplish your specific goals within the short-term period, medium-term period or long-term period.

When planning within the short-term frame, you should be looking at your needs and goals for the next two years or so.

When thinking of your goals within the medium-term, you can look at the period from two to five years. Or you could even look at your goals with a ten-year frame.

The long-term period extends beyond ten years.

You will have to look at your financial goals according to your target amount of money and time. This should also include your commitment.

When you are trying to accomplish a particular goal, that would mean setting and determining the number of days, weeks and months necessary so that you can reach your specific money goals.

How much amount of dollars do you think you will be able to set aside for savings?

You will have to be specific about the period of time it covers. When will you begin and until when will you do this? This should specify a set of dates.

Remember each goal has to have a particular plan of action.

Let us say, if your financial goal is to have savings (or emergency fund) with the amount of six thousand dollars ($6000) within a period of twenty-four (24) months, your financial plan should look like our example here:

Short-term Period: Two Years
Goal: $6000.00
Amount of Funds to Set Aside Monthly: $250.00
Number of Months to Accomplish:
24 months
Date to Begin Your Commitment:
December 31, 2020
Target Date to Use the Funds: December 31, 2022

* * *

REVISIT YOUR FINANCIAL GOALS

It is important to revisit your financial needs and goals as many times as you could in a year. The strategy is to determine how things are going and analyze your personal financial accomplishment.

You should understand well your view of your financial situation.

Is your opinion about money based on your actual need or have other people influenced you in setting your goals?

Do you try to accomplish your plan based on what your neighbours might have owned or might have bought recently? Have you attempted to try to be of the same level, if not compete, with your neighbours' or friends' material possessions?

In other words, are your personal financial priorities based on social influences or other people's opinions?

Have you thought about whether your goals qualify as a 'need'? Do you urgently need to fulfill these things? Or can your goals be categorized as the things that you simply desire and want to have?

How about the current economy? Does the current market affect the way you set your goals?

The idea in creating your strategic approach to manage money is for you to assess and reflect upon your actual needs.

There may be some influences around you, but remember, at the end of the day, you are responsible for the financial decisions that you make.

What would be the impact of your choices and decisions? Are you prepared to take the risks that could result from your decisions?

You must base your financial goals on the income you make, the amount of money you can save and the amount of money you spend to pay for all of your financial obligations.

Can your financial resources meet your financial needs and goals?

Can you think of and identify your current financial needs and look into your financial goals for the short-term period, medium-term period, and long-term-period? What do you think would be your strategic financial plan?

* * *

PHASE 3: What Financial Strategies or Options Do You Have?

It is vital to know and understand what available financial options you have. Usually, when making decisions, we try to examine several alternatives and possibilities. We also try to see the pros and cons of each available option. In this way, you will be aware of the possible outcomes.

Your options or strategies may include one or a combination of the 4Ms:

Maintain Your Strategy

Go in the same direction you are doing, providing you find the strategy still practical and applicable.

Magnify Your Strategy

You can increase the degree, level or amount of money that you set aside each month.

Modify Your Strategy

You may opt to adjust or alter some aspects of your strategy.

For example, you can choose to transfer some funds from your savings account to a GIC (Guaranteed Investment Certificate) or term deposit account if you think you could earn better interest rates.

Make a Better Strategy

As you become familiar with various strategies, you may find that things are becoming a bit easier to handle.

In the process, you could think of a more appropriate strategy.

For example, when you receive additional money, it would make sense to consider what form the money would work best in terms of return.

Depending on your goal, you may have other considerations.

What is your priority at this point? Build savings? Pay off your high-interest credit card debt? Or put money into your emergency fund?

What would be your resources?

You can earn extra funds through a part-time job. Or you may want to use any amount of money from your bonus, commission, or incentives (that you have earned), depending on the type of job you do. And if it would be possible, any amount from your tax refund.

CHOOSING AND DECIDING ON STRATEGIES

Choosing the best option or strategy or a combination of strategies would depend on how you view your financial situation.

The worst thing that one could do is not to think through all of the options available before acting upon a certain decision.

All of the strategies may not probably work in every situation. However, when given some choices, you will have to choose the best strategy according to your financial situation.

Deciding on a particular course of action can result in some risks. However, the ability to be creative when making financial decisions is a huge responsibility in itself.

When you exercise your ability to come up with well-thought-out decisions, you are doing a great favour to yourself. That is, achieving something one step at a time.

Sooner or later, you would be ready to take upon the next huge steps.

Then you will find yourself becoming more comfortable and effective with your decision-making ability.

PHASE 4: Assess your options. Are these feasible?

At this point, you will now go through the process of choosing (and deciding on) your financial strategies.

Would this be feasible in your financial situation?

What is the impact of the current global, national, and local economic condition?

Do you have any members in the family that depend on you?

How would your dependents be affected by your choices, decisions, and actions? Would you be willing to give up certain luxuries and extravagant celebrations? Would your financial strategies go well with your beliefs and values?

Are you confident that you can carry out the financial activities that are part of your financial strategies?

Are you prepared for a life-changing sound financial experience?

When you make a financial decision, you will realize that there are certain sacrifices that you must be willing to undertake.

For example, if you are to do a second job that requires at least four hours a day or twenty hours a week, it could mean giving up that number of hours that you used to enjoy on other personal activities. That is, in exchange for earning additional money that could help meet your savings goal.

Another example that you could give up is the time and money associated with expensive out-of-town vacations. That will be, in exchange for your financial goal to save up for a down payment, so that you could buy your first apartment or single-detached home.

Looking at the scenarios, you will recognize that there are opportunities, as well as sacrifices, and other things (that may equate to time or money, or even both time and money) that you are giving up (that may be of significant value to you).

The process of making personal financial decisions would be a constant day-to-day activity. Time will come that you will realize, going through such a process would be much easier with your determination and commitment.

Ultimately, that will form part of your whole new approach to your daily living.

If you are determined to accomplish a sound financial plan, then you must acknowledge some opportunities and sacrifices that must come with your decisions.

Can you think of and identify what opportunities and sacrifices (that relate to time or money) you would be open and willing to undertake, considering your financial goals?

* * *

UNDERSTANDING AND ASSESSING RISKS

There could be some risks involved when you go through the process of financial decision-making. You must understand that it would not be easy to recognize risks and even more challenging to assess risks.

Financial decision-making can be a complex task. But you can find a way to simplify the process.

The most practical way to learn about a particular risk is to research and gather information. That could come from your own experience or experience of others, such as a member of your family, a relative, or a friend. You could also do some research online.

You could obtain more information about personal financial planning. You could also seek professional help, if necessary.

Your goal should be to be familiar with the risks that may result from certain financial decisions.

Now, let us look at some possible financial risks.

When you look at the global, national and local economic factors, you will notice that risks are associated with inflation, market prices and interest rates.

Of course, these risks may have different levels of impact to every person. Risks would depend on each individual circumstance.

As you evaluate your financial options or a combination of your financial strategies, you will realize that your decisions can affect many aspects of your personal situation.

Risks may be associated with your current investments and assets, income and employment, and many other personal risks, such as health and safety.

Risks Involved with Money, Investments and Assets

When you think about the activities that you do with money, investments, and assets, what risks could you see or encounter?

Before you decide in which form of investment you would put your money, it would make sense to assess the terms and conditions associated with the investment.

You must also assess whether potential earnings would be worth the length of time it will take to liquidate the asset. This is very important, particularly, if you would need to access some funds at some point.

Also, you have to understand that market conditions can affect various financial situations, which at times, could mean getting lower return, lower market value or price.

In some instances, you could lose a significant value of your money when you decide to purchase or sell your assets and investments.

Risks Involved with Income, Job and Employment

Changes in employment and job circumstances can affect personal lifestyle. It could mean revisiting the way you spend and save money.

People may not easily be comfortable with lifestyle changes. It would, therefore, make sense to prepare for some possible changes. For example, you could set aside some considerable amount of money (or what you call your savings) while still employed. In the event of an unexpected employment gap, you will have some funds that can help you get back on your feet as you prepare to find other job prospects.

Such changes may also entail acquiring new skills or enhancing your knowledge in your chosen field. Or this may call for starting a new small business and getting into self-employment.

Every decision you make in many situations will always have risks and consequences. It is imperative that you become familiar with the possible risks and challenges that can impact your outlook and lifestyle.

Personal, Health and Safety Risks

When you evaluate your financial decisions, you will notice that your taste and preference could affect your well-being. It could even lead to a not so favourable situation. For example, some people would prefer to buy organic products as opposed to non-organic products. Most often than not, organic products may cost a lot more than the non-organic products. When you are going through a life-changing financial decision, it could mean giving up the more expensive organic products and deciding to buy the non-organic, instead.

Another example is changing brand preferences, like buying generic products, instead of the branded products. When you are used to a particular brand, then all of a sudden you come up with the decision to switch to another low-cost brand, you could be giving up some aspects of your personal taste or lifestyle.

The trade-off may have an impact on health and personal enjoyment.

Where to Obtain Information Sources

It is important to recognize that having appropriate financial information is fundamental in order to come up with the best financial decisions possible.

Deciding to embrace a new personal lifestyle, which can affect your social and financial conditions, will entail growing your financial knowledge and enhancing your acquired skills. We are in the digital age in which easy access to information is readily available. Information about developing your understanding of personal finance may be obtained through a variety of print and media sources, such as: books, e-books, newspapers, magazines, videos, podcasts, and even radio and television programs. Digital media also could present many vital information sources. You can search online to find helpful personal finance websites and social media sites. You can also subscribe to blogs, newsfeeds, and even cellphone apps.

In addition, many financial experts, banks, as well as real estate and financial organizations conduct workshops, seminars and other educational courses and learning programs. Such programs can give participants better understanding on certain personal finance issues and topics. Many of the seminars and programs may be offered free.

You must find out though whether these would fit your learning objectives to achieve your financial goals.

PHASE 5: Develop, Write and Execute Your Financial Action Plan

At this point, you must have a checklist of the things or information you could include in your financial action plan.

To continue with phase 5, you must have reflected upon and answered the questions from Phase 1 to Phase 4.

Phase 1: Where are you at this point? Understand Your Personal Financial Position

Phase 2: What Are Your Financial Needs and Goals: Know How You Can Accomplish Your Objectives

Phase 3: What Financial Options Do You Have?

Phase 4: Assess Your Options. Are These Feasible?

Working on a financial plan involves identifying clearly concrete steps to accomplish your goals and ultimately, fulfilling your financial needs.

For example, your short-term goal is to have $2000.00 savings by the end of December of the current year.

If you start your savings goal on the 31st of March, you can look at 10 equal contributions of $200.00.

$200.00 = March 31st
$200.00 = April 30th
$200.00 = May 31st
$200.00 = June 30th
$200.00 = July 31st
$200.00 = August 31st
$200.00 = September 30th
$200.00 = October 31st
$200.00 = November 30th
$200.00 = December 31st

$2000.00 = Total Savings

Another strategy you might want to consider, depending on your situation, is to get a part-time job or other means that can help increase your total income.

In some instances, you would need professional help to work on your financial concerns in areas such as tax, insurance, retirement, investments, credit and loans.

As you complete one specific short-term financial goal, you would then start to look into the next set of financial goals in line.

Remember, your goals must come in the order of importance or priority. It is your task to decide which of your goals must come first. You are responsible for the outcome of your decisions. You must decide according to your needs and assess any possible consequences of your choices.

Creating a sound financial plan will require that you understand the need to have self-control and discipline with your financial budget. It boils down to focusing on your financial goals and identifying the most appropriate strategies.

Each financial plan would look different to every individual. However, some common factors generally affect financial planning.

* * *

GUIDING QUESTIONS TO
DEVELOP FINANCIAL PLAN

Here are some of the questions that will help guide you in developing your financial plan:

- Is your financial plan flexible?
- Does your financial plan allow ease of access?
- Does your financial plan have guidelines on safety and security?
- Does your financial plan allow you to look at earnings, taxes, and savings?

Carrying Out Your Financial Plan

Creating a personal financial plan requires commitment and focus. Without the required discipline to put the steps into action, the plan that was originally developed will not be effective.

It is not to say though that everything will absolutely go as planned. There are, of course, certain situations that would necessitate changes in your action plan. The idea here is to be able to oversee where your financial direction is going. This would include tracking your financial resources and activities. How was your spending? How much savings can you make for the current month? Are you earning enough income? Are you able to pay your debts and settle your monthly financial obligations? Are you on track in meeting your immediate financial goals? How do you view your long-term goals?

It is important to remember that your plan is a process to accomplish your goal.

Do not overwhelm yourself with what you have written in your plan. You can simply look at it as a guiding map to reach your destination.

You have got to trust yourself and go on for the right reasons. Your motivation to succeed financially will arm you every step of the way.

There are times, though, you may encounter challenges that you may not foresee.

And you may get lost in the process. You will need to find your direction back to where you are going.

How you overcome challenges and obstacles will make a difference in carrying out your plan. At times, you may need to take a different direction in order to reach your destination.

With the plan that you have developed, you have several possibilities and choices that might be appropriate.

Remember, your financial plan could include sets of contingency plans (or what we call emergency plans) to allow some changes and adjustments, as may be necessary.

The bottom line is getting through and achieving your goals. You can do this with your focus and determination.

* * *

PLANNING AND CREATING YOUR BUDGET

The process of planning and creating a budget will entail a systematic set of activities and guidelines.

The **first step** is to create a balance sheet that will outline your current financial situation, which will include your assets and liabilities.

What are the sources of your wealth? Where does your money go? How would you assess your current financial health?

The **second step** is to determine your specific goals. This will include your short-term goals and long-term goals. Focus on one goal at a time. Choose carefully the financial goals that you will need to prioritize. How much money would it require? Make sure that your goal is within your allotted budget.

The **third step** is to create your financial action plan. Make sure that you are spending according to your targeted budget.

The **fourth step** is to execute your financial plan. You will take charge and make things happen.

PHASE 6: Evaluate, Adjust and Rework Your Action Plan

The final phase would require that you reassess your personal financial situation. Do you see any progress? Have you achieved your desired financial goals based on your budget? If not, you can review your plan.

What other options and strategies could you make? Which part of your plan do you need to change? Do you need to magnify, modify or make better strategies? Try to see the bigger picture.

NEED FOR FURTHER RESEARCH

Some personal financial situations would necessitate further research.

We benefit a lot by looking at various surveys and other useful financial information.

We are in a digital age in which we could have access to several web and mobile technologies.

If you are using a smartphone or a tablet, you can browse through some personal finance applications that can allow you to compare products and prices and even organize and manage your financial activities.

Banks and financial institutions can provide access to financial information through their websites and mobile applications. They can also provide access to online calculators to give consumers information on loan payments, including principal and interest.

When looking at financial information, try to see if you could find something that would be of use to you (or your current situation). Or you could do the opposite.

Try to observe how the financial information and example that you see would differ from your financial position. Could you apply, or in some cases, modify your financial strategies? Review other information that may be necessary.

REVIEWING AND REASSESSING
YOUR FINANCIAL PLAN

It is important to note that reviewing and reassessing your financial plan is a cycle that keeps revolving. It does not end. The good thing is you will be good at it as you keep your financial goals in mind. You will remain focused. You may periodically review your financial plan. You may do an annual review of your finances. Or you may do it as often as necessary.

If you foresee possible changes in your financial circumstance, you may need to do more frequent audits. You may also have to look at other contributing factors that may affect your financial situation. That will include the global, national and local market conditions, as well as various social factors. When you experience some life changes that will have an impact on your current financial position, the financial planning process that you have gone through can help you adjust to those changes. It will help to point you towards your financial priorities that need more urgent attention.

Finally, you will be confident that your financial needs and goals would be in a better position as you tackle each goal at a time.

FIVE

ACHIEVING SAVINGS GOALS

Achieving Savings Goals

CHAPTER FIVE

- Personal Thoughts about Money
- Determining your Money Habits and Lifestyle
- Embracing Change, New Habits and Skills
- Challenges with Saving Money
- Finding Answers to Important Questions about Saving Money
- How Will You Save Money
- Saving Money is a Creative Process
- Pay Yourself First
- Your Financial Goal and Savings Plan
- When Will You Begin Saving?
- Decide Where to Save Money
- Making Money Work for You
- Have you heard about the Rule of 72?
- Saving Money versus Investing Money
- How Values Shape Your Planning to Save and Spend

ACHIEVING SAVINGS GOALS

We could all agree that the process of saving money is essential to achieving your financial fitness.

When you try to accomplish your savings goals, you would be doing the necessary steps to fulfill what matters to you most, achieving a sense of financial security, responsibility, and independence.

Sometimes, it does not matter whether these financial goals would require a big or small amount of dollars as long as you are in charge, you take control, and you (know how to) put matters in their proper order.

It is the personal lifestyle and behaviour towards handling money that would make a real difference.

PERSONAL THOUGHTS ABOUT MONEY

When we were at a very young age, we all loved to dream many fancy things. And we even wish or think of some impossible things to happen as though we are in a fairy tale. We all have our respective share of memories about wanting to have something.

And there were certain things that would require some amount of money in order to get what we wanted.

Kids have the tendency to be impulsive. They don't understand how adults handle things. However, kids mimic what they see.

Do you still remember your response every time you would ask for something that you like very much, and yet you were not able to get that thing? Do you recall the explanation given to you at the time?

It could be that for financial reasons, your parents refused to give what you wanted. Or it could be that you were asking for something - that your parents think - you do not really need, after all.

During the time, were there circumstances that you heard grown-ups discuss money issues or problems?

When was the first time you came to consciously think and understand about money and what it really means to you?

What lessons might have you learned based on your early memories about money – about receiving money, about spending money and saving money?

How do you relate this experience to your financial lifestyle today?

How has it formed your habits on spending and saving money?

DETERMINING YOUR
MONEY HABITS AND LIFESTYLE

When you hear the word money, what would automatically come to your mind? How do you feel about money? How do you react if and when you receive money unexpectedly? Do you get excited and think about the things that you want to buy? Or do you feel that there will never be enough money coming into your pocket?

Every person has a different approach to spending and saving money. How do you describe your current money habits and lifestyle?

Are you an impulsive spender and not able to manage and control spending triggers?

Are you a fun-killer who would rather put all money in savings – as if not enough money would come into your pocket?

Are you a big spender and want to create attention and admiration of others? Are you willing to spend money at all cost for the sake of maintaining a certain image?

Are you spending money to give pleasure and get affection from some people? Do you find it hard to say no to others who ask for things?

Are you looking forward to saving more and not wanting to experience money problems that you had experienced in the past? Are you thinking of planning and preparing your budget carefully before spending?

Are you a disciplined saver yet you are aware of financial priorities and the importance of balanced spending and having good fun at the same time?

Knowing what kind of money habits you have will help you understand how you will approach your plan. How about the lifestyle of the people in your household, your spouse, your children, your parents? How do they influence you?

Do you like the way you regard money?

EMBRACING CHANGE, NEW HABITS AND SKILLS

Do you worry about your future? Do you foresee some changes to your circumstance? If so, now is the best time to acknowledge your situation.

As you form new money habits and lifestyle, it would be good to consider your strengths and skills. The same way, it is imperative to consider your weaknesses and other skills you need to develop.

You could use some of your skills when deciding to save money. It would help to develop skills, such as: goal-setting, organizing, planning, scheduling, controlling, managing, researching, communicating, and many other skills.

Can you associate which skills you have that can be useful in managing your finances?

* * *

CHALLENGES WITH SAVING MONEY

Deciding to save money is not an easy task. You may even encounter temptations along the way. You will find things that will catch your attention and that will trigger you to use your money.

Most people would agree that it is always a lot easier to spend money.

Therefore, the idea of saving requires that you exercise self-control.

Remind yourself of your goal and the things (that you have declared to yourself) you are willing to give up. It will help you to focus on your savings goal.

When you think of your financial priorities, and you develop good spending behaviour and habits, you will find that saving money, after all, is about an attitude. That would help you keep on track with your plan.

Finding Answers to Important Questions about Saving Money

Another challenge that you might experience with saving money is the ability to ask important questions.

How will I save money?

When will I be able to begin?

Where would I put my savings?

How often could I contribute to my savings plan?

How Will You Save Money

For several obvious reasons, many people find saving money quite challenging to accomplish. However, with a strong desire and commitment to achieve financial success, saving money is, after all, a very vital task.

There are different ways in which you could start your savings plan.

For example, instead of spending $2.00 for a hot beverage, you can opt into preparing your own at home. Can you imagine how much money you could save a month? If you're looking at about 5 days a week for 52 weeks, then that would be like $520.00 a year.

$2.00 x 5 days = $10.00/week

$10.00/week x 52 weeks = $520.00/year

Saving Money is a Creative Process

If you come to think of it, saving money is a creative process, which involves expense reduction and debt elimination, as well as choosing better options to keep more money in your pocket and pursuing other activities that would generate more income.

How should a person decide between the idea of saving money and spending money? Of course, the thought about spending money (to comply with financial obligations) is equally necessary, as (the idea of) saving money.

What you are trying to do here, though, is to MAKE SAVING MONEY a priority.

Let us face it, for most people, saving money is not a day-to-day activity. Many people tend to ignore things related to personal finance for varied reasons.

Therefore it is fundamental to declare consciously to yourself that you would like to BEGIN SAVING MONEY.

You can do this by declaring that you would need to pay yourself first.

You probably must have heard a long time ago about this strategy from other financial experts or sources. And guess what, this strategy helps in putting your savings goals in line.

Pay Yourself First

How do you do paying yourself first?

When you decide to pay yourself first, that means you will need to set aside some funds or a portion of your earnings that is ideally about ten to twenty percent (10% to 20%) before allocating the money for other expenses.

If you find the strategy a bit difficult in your situation at this point, you can try to begin allocating at least five percent (5%). Then you can gradually increase to ten percent (10%).

What counts more is for you to start with your savings plan.

* * *

YOUR FINANCIAL GOAL AND SAVINGS PLAN

To make your savings plan effective and successful, you will need to focus on your financial goals. Always think about your concrete goal. Paying yourself first can help you accomplish this - one goal at a time.

Make it simple. Do not make things complicated for you. And make sure it is achievable. Otherwise, you will need to be even more creative. Or think of other ways you can accomplish your plan.

It is of paramount importance to remain focused. And stick to your plan.

In some unexpected events, it is but all right to adjust, depending on how you are going.

Remember, a plan is only a guide. You are the creator of your goals. And you can always re-work your process, depending on how you are working out.

Just be sure that despite the odds that you might encounter along the way, you're able to re-direct your path towards your planned destination.

WHEN WILL YOU BEGIN SAVING?

Deciding when to begin saving is a personal matter. However, it is always best to begin as early as possible – which means NOW.

In fact, the longer you delay, the more you could be missing out on opportunities. Even putting aside a small amount of money now can help over time and contribute to your future financial goals.

Attaining financial independence requires hard work. That would include familiarizing yourself with financial concepts and increasing your knowledge in saving money. After all, no one is born knowing how to manage finances.

People learn and develop skills as they age. People gather information and learn from other experiences.

Saving and investing your money over a period of time would necessitate a long-term commitment. It is not just a one-shot deal and then the person forgets.

DECIDE WHERE TO SAVE MONEY

Knowing where to save money is an important factor that would contribute to your overall savings goals.

When doing your banking or opening a bank account, you must choose the right bank or financial institution that would best serve your needs.

Be familiar with your local banks and what financial products they offer. Banks often have online presence that you could visit as you research and decide on which bank could be right for you.

Know the bank fees, interest rates and investment products. Some financial institutions, like certain credit unions, for example, do not charge bank fees on basic chequing account.

On the other hand, you must understand and assess how other banks can help meet your expectations.

Which bank can help you increase the value of your money faster in terms of interest rate on savings?

Which bank does not cost you much to maintain your savings account?

Which bank allows you to contribute to your savings account more easily?

Can you automate your saving schedule?

Banks offer various financial products. In Canada, most banks offer ways you could open and maintain registered accounts (for RRSP or registered retirement savings plan) and non-registered (or open) accounts.

Consumers can choose from GICs (guaranteed investment certificates) or term deposit accounts, and high-interest savings accounts. Other savvy investors would put some money in mutual funds, bonds, ETFs (exchange-traded funds), stocks and even real estate, depending on how well they understand the different forms of investments.

If you are a new investor, it would be better for you to consider and look to investment options that you know and understand well.

However, you can always increase your knowledge about other investment options. You can talk to a professional, read books, and understand many other financial concepts.

You should be able to weigh the pros and cons of each of the investment possibilities.

Do not decide and sign on something that is not clear to you. In other words, learn to protect yourself with your investments. After all, they are your hard-earned money.

MAKING MONEY WORK FOR YOU

When you are preparing for your savings goal plan, it is a good thing to consider not just the amount of money you need to set aside and save for the future but how you can grow your money as well.

There are many ways in which your savings can increase in value over time. Unless, of course, you opt into keeping your money in your bedroom, then there's no way you would make your money earn extra for you.

The idea of 'making your money work for you' would seem desirable. Even if you just keep your money in the bank - in the form of high interest savings or term deposit - and without doing much work, you will find that your money could earn a decent return for you, depending on the interest rates.

You can opt into some term deposits that can give you an option to look into rising interest rates each year. It pays to know where you will park your money while you are saving for your future goals.

Let us say you have five hundred ($500) dollars sitting somewhere, not doing anything for you. And then you put that money in a high-interest savings account that would let you earn three percent (3%) interest per year. As a result, you would then earn some fifteen dollars ($15.00) from that money on the first year of the term. Without doing much on your part and by simply parking it in your high-interest bearing account, you would have a total of five-hundred fifteen dollars ($515.00) at the end of the year. If you look at the amount of fifteen dollars ($15.00), you will find that it is not much of a significant amount.

However, the amount could grow more if you keep it in your account for a long time, and even more if you add some tens, or hundreds, or thousands. That is how your money savings could grow over time.

You probably must have heard about the concept of compound interest.

It is the money (or the amount of interest) you have earned from the interest.

Year 1 $500.00 x 3% = $15.00
Year 2 $515.00 x 3% = $15.45
Year 3 $530.45 x 3% = $15.91
Year 4 $546.36 x 3% = $16.39
Year 5 $562.75 x 3% = $16.88
Total Savings after Year 5
= 579.63 or $580.00 (rounded off)

You will have earned the amount seventy-nine dollars and sixty-three cents ($79.63) equivalent to the compound interest of fifteen point ninety-two percent (15.92%) based on three percent (3%) rate per year.

The longer you keep the money in your account, the higher amount you will earn. If you keep your savings for more than twenty (20) years or even more, you will have substantial value.

You must note that the figures (that we have just discussed) are for illustration purposes. Of course, you can use the actual amount that you have. Be it one thousand (1000), ten thousand (10,000), or one hundred thousand (100,000).

HAVE YOU HEARD ABOUT
THE RULE OF 72?

The concept tells you how fast you can let your money double in value if kept in an interest-generating account. This concept clearly illustrates how the power of compound interest will help you to double your money or your savings over time.

You are looking at two things here. The first thing is, knowing the length of time it will take to double your money. And the second thing is at what rate you would need your money to earn.

For example, in our earlier scenario, if you keep five hundred dollars ($500) in an account that lets you earn three percent (3%) interest rate per year, and you apply the Rule of Seventy-Two (72), it will take twenty-four (24) years to double your money.

Now, if you prefer to make your money work even harder for you and allow it to double in twelve (12) years, instead of twenty-four (24) years, you will need to have an interest rate twice the three percent (3%), which is six percent (6%) interest rate.

How do you calculate using the *Rule of 72?*
Simply divide 72 by the interest rate.

If the interest rate is three percent (3%), we divide seventy-two (72) by three (3), and you will arrive with the number twenty-four (24). That would be equivalent to the total number of years it will take to have your original amount of five hundred dollars ($500.00) to double.

Another way to apply the Rule of Seventy-Two (72), as explained earlier in our example, is to save and leave the money for twelve (12) years at an interest rate of six percent (6%). The formula is to simply divide seventy-two (72) by twelve (12) and you would get the required interest rate of six percent (6%).

Now, can you imagine the scenario in which you keep adding each year on to your savings?

The more consistent you could add money onto your savings, the higher the value you would generate and the quicker your savings would increase.

The earlier you could prepare your savings goal plan, and the sooner you can implement your financial activities, the more savvy and secure you would be with your finances.

Procrastinating to plan to save money can seriously affect your savings goals. You may find it a bit challenging to catch up.

Learning to apply the concept of the power of compound interest and the Rule of Seventy-Two (72) is the beginning of a long-term process.

Acquiring financial knowledge is what it takes to begin the process of successfully becoming financially independent.

SAVING MONEY

VERSUS

INVESTING MONEY

It is important to remember that saving money and investing money are not synonymous.

When we look at saving money, we look at the means to put our money in the safest form. In this way, we would be able to access it if and when we need it, given the time and terms that go with it.

Your goal here is to preserve your hard-earned money at a reasonable interest rate or at the highest interest rate it can earn.

Banks have savings products that offer customers to keep their money through various forms, such as savings accounts, chequing accounts, and term deposits or GICs (guaranteed investment certificates).

Maintaining savings with such bank products usually would come with a low yield or interest rate.

When you put your money in various forms of investments, such as stocks, you would find that some investment instruments can produce higher returns. Yet, they could be risky.

When you are in the beginning stage of organizing your finances, your goals should be to pay off any loans, or credit cards, and any other debts.

Then, it would be imperative to build your emergency fund. You may need to access it in an unforeseeable future, such as when you lose your job and any other things and events that may require urgent funds.

Next, of course, is to allocate funds for short-term goals. You would be looking at your financial needs that would require the use of money in the next few months to probably twelve (12) months or even up to twenty-four (24) months. You would need to be able to access such funds if and when necessary.

Some people look to invest funds that can generate better returns over a period of time that can mean many, many years. The aim is to allow the funds to work and grow within the longer-term period. In other words, access to funds may not be the immediate concern.

However, if there's one important thing one must remember about investments is that 'putting money in certain investment forms' can result in some risks and loss of money.

Investors should know the level of risk they can manage and how comfortable they are with their investing strategies. When you know what you are doing, investing your money could be a good thing.

With investing, you have a greater chance of gaining more money, most especially when things work well.

As a new investor, it is imperative that you become familiar with investing approaches, grow your knowledge about various investment instruments and find resources to help you keep learning. You should know the concepts related to mutual funds, stocks or securities, exchange-traded funds or ETFs, and other forms of financial investments.

You may need to consult with an investment consultant and do your independent research as well. Do not rely on just one source. You will need to learn more about how stock investing works and how risky it could be to invest in each security.

The best advice there is – BE WELL-INFORMED!

Owning investments can be exciting, especially if you're looking at a higher return, but there's also the risk that you could lose your hard-earned money. The best advice there is – BE WELL-INFORMED!

How about investing money in real estate?

Investing in real estate is investing money in a different context.

When you are buying a home, you have two goals in line here. First, you can use the home as your dwelling. You can decide to live in your home as long as you want. Then, of course, when you sell your home, you would then receive some funds as proceeds from the sale of your property, the value of which is equivalent to the equity that you have built over some period of time.

Depending on how the real estate market goes, buying and selling could serve a variety of purposes. Make sure that you know the reasons why you want to buy or sell a piece of property. And this would require appropriate planning.

Talk to real estate professionals to learn about your options and to better prepare for your adventure in real estate buying and selling.

You may need to consult with a team of professionals, such as a real estate agent, independent mortgage broker or bank mortgage officer, home inspector, appraiser, and lawyer. Make sure that you work with the consultants that you can trust. You can ask questions and clarify issues or wordings that you don't understand.

You may want to conduct your independent research as well.

Remember, at the end of the day, you are responsible for all the decisions that you make. And it is your hard-earned money that is at stake.

HOW VALUES SHAPE YOUR
PLANNING TO SAVE AND SPEND

Personal values, family values, and cultural values influence the way people spend money.

It is imperative to put the idea about saving and spending money with the proper perspective.

For example, if a family considers owning a home an ultimate goal, then a savings goal will be focused on saving up for a down payment and other home-buying costs. Some people would pursue goals, such as taking further studies and taking their dream vacations. Others look into pursuing entrepreneurship. And so on.

Whatever it is that you believe would matter to you, it is vital that you plan carefully. Consider financial resources available and assess whether these would match with your financial goals. Adjust or strategize, if necessary.

People have different influences and have different values.

We learn wisdom from our experiences. We acquire our values and beliefs from the people that surround us, our parents, our siblings, our relatives, our friends, our teachers, our associates, and our colleagues.

Up to what extent do we allow others to influence our way of thinking and behaviour?

The answer to that would depend on a lot of factors. We need to be able to emphasize up to what point we can be comfortable. Some people would follow the same values all along, while others embrace new values.

Can you clarify what values matter to you at this point? How do these values relate to your savings goals?

The moment you recognize your values, you should determine whether your spending relates to a real need or a nice-to-have or nice-to-do kind of expense.

Focusing on realistic goals should drive you to set aside some money for savings. The idea is to put money aside regularly for specific savings goals.

There are many ways in which you could contribute to your savings plan. When you are determined and motivated, you could always find ways to be creative with your approaches in money-saving matters.

SIX

CREATING A HEALTHY SAVINGS MIX

Creating a Healthy Savings Mix

CHAPTER SIX

- Creating a Healthy Savings Mix: Making Your SMART Goal
- How Do You Know You Are Achieving Your Goal?
- Can You Attain Your Goals?
- Self-Image, Confidence and Opportunities
- Do You Find Your Goal Reasonable, Relevant and Realistic?
- Does Your Goal Have a Deadline?
- What Are You Saving For?

CREATING A HEALTHY SAVINGS MIX:
MAKING YOUR SMART GOAL

When you are creating a mix for your savings, you go back to the very first steps of the process. That would be knowing your situation and your financial priorities. That means you will have to review and set your goals according to your assessment of your needs.

You probably have heard about the acronym 'SMART' when it comes to planning and goal-setting.

Simply put, you must describe your goals as specific, measurable, attainable, reasonable (or realistic), and time-based.

When we say a goal must be specific, we refer to a particular target.

For example, when someone says: "I want to lose weight," the person is referring to a general goal, which may, or may not, happen.

But then, a person could state the goal with more concrete details.

"I want to lose weight. Therefore, I would need to go to the [CoreFitNext] gym every week for twelve weeks to lose ten (10) pounds. I need to spend time starting next week, which means giving up my one-hour video game time." Then the person is now referring to a specific goal.

If you notice, a specific goal responds to the "W" questions:

WHO – Who is doing the activity to achieve the goal? In our example, it is obvious that "I" (or the person who intends to reach the goal) is the one doing the activity.

WHAT – What is that particular thing or activity that needed to be accomplished? Referring to our previous example, that would be: "go to the gym."

WHY – Why do I need to accomplish this activity? The person stated, "to lose ten (10) pounds."

WHERE – Where do I need to be, or to go, to accomplish the particular activity? In our example, the person stated: "CoreFitNext gym."

WHEN – When do I need to do it, and how often? In our example, the time frame or period was stated: "every week for twelve weeks... starting next week."

WHICH – Which are the things I need to give up so that I could achieve this goal? Or the ways or requirements in which I have to consider so I could fulfill this need? In here, the person identifies, "giving up my one-hour video game time."

Our goal must be specific so that there is a greater chance of achieving success.

Our goal must be specific
so that there is a greater chance of
achieving success.

Accomplishing your savings goal would require writing a
declaration (of what you want to achieve, what you need
to do, and how to do it). You may want to write it in a way
that is similar to our example.

*Can you think and identify your specific financial
goal?*

* * *

HOW DO YOU KNOW YOU ARE ACHIEVING
YOUR GOAL?

How do we know if a goal is measurable?

At this point, there has to be some sort of criteria in
which to measure how we are doing.

Do you see improvement from the time you started on
your activity? How far or how close are you to attaining
your goal?

Remember, you should be able to measure how well
you are doing.

You set your standard so that you know if you are on
track or falling behind.

Some questions that could help in keeping track of your development - should have answers that you can quantify or calculate.

You can ask the following: *How much money should I set aside weekly (or monthly, whichever is convenient)?*

How many weeks (or months) should I set aside such an amount?

If I fall behind with my savings contribution, how much more money should I set aside, or how many more weeks (or months) should I save so that I could make up and reach my targeted goal?

You will notice that with your savings goal, there must be a target date and target amount of savings. In that way, you can accomplish a certain amount of money at a particular time.

You would know if you are on your way to fulfilling your goal or if you need to adjust your strategy - by extending the number of weeks or months, or if you need to double the amount of money you set aside for savings.

Knowing the necessary steps and strategies could help guide you in adjusting or reworking your financial plan.

* * *

CAN YOU ATTAIN YOUR GOALS?

Knowing and establishing a specific goal is one thing. Ensuring that a goal is measurable is another thing. Now, do you believe that you can achieve this?

Do you have a positive feeling about your plan?

Are you confident that you possess a strong drive and motivation?

What are the skills and abilities that you have that can help you accomplish your financial activities?

Do you have financial capacity? Do you have some source of income that can help you set aside money regularly?

What are the things that you need to give up (so that you can focus on what is more important to you at this point)? In other words, how committed are you?

You can reach any goal when you think of concrete steps and create a schedule that enables you to carry out your plan.

You would get one step closer to achieving your goal as you take on one step at a time. You would become more empowered and focused.

You would have a better view of yourself.

Can you think and figure out ways so that you can realize your goal?

* * *

SELF-IMAGE, CONFIDENCE AND OPPORTUNITIES

Your self-image mirrors your confidence. Each day that you feel good about yourself (and your decisions), you develop and grow your level of confidence. As a result, you can become as creative as you can be with your approach in life. Ideas will keep flowing onto your head. And you start to think of opportunities from many angles.

You may look at opportunities that you may have disregarded or even things that you may not have tried yet. For example, if it costs you more to drive a car (given the high gas prices and the cost to maintain a car), you could opt to do carpooling or take a bus to get to your office or place of destination. In this way, you can contribute more to your savings from the money that you can save from giving up driving.

You can do many other ways to add to your savings. For example, if you are used to buying some snacks on your way to work, you can decide to make your sandwich or snacks before leaving home.

Also, if you are used to buying expensive meals for your lunch or dinner, you can prepare your version of your favorite meals. Yes, you might need to do extra work and set aside some time to prepare meals. But the payoff is giving up spending money. In effect, this can help you add to your savings contribution.

As a result, you become more determined to seek and find more opportunities – which could be a money-saving opportunity or an income opportunity.

And each time you see your way through, you become more confident about yourself.

You would become more confident of the decisions that you make.

You start to realize that you are getting closer.

You recognize that by giving up certain things or temporary enjoyment, you are on your way to accomplishing a better life – a financially independent life.

Can you think and identify ways you can save money with your day-to-day activities?

* * *

DO YOU FIND YOUR GOAL
REASONABLE, RELEVANT AND REALISTIC?

How committed and capable are you in working on your goal?

Sometimes, people prepare a plan, then do some other things. After a while, they lose track.

And why does that happen?

The reason being, goals are not realistic. Remember, it takes a process. It takes dedication. And most importantly, it takes hard work.

You know when a goal is reasonable when you can relate it to your available financial resources as well as your knowledge of how to go about the necessary steps on a particular deadline.

Are you in a position to work on your plan? How would you allocate your time? How willing and able are you to accomplish this? Is your goal practical in your situation?

It is okay to set high goals as long as you believe you are able to do what it takes to accomplish the necessary steps. No one can tell if a goal is realistic and achievable, but you. After all, you know what you're capable of doing, what you're capable of giving up and what you're capable of achieving in the long run.

The goal should inspire you - making financial activity appear seamless and achievable, despite its difficulty, because you believe in what you are doing and in what you are trying to accomplish.

DOES YOUR GOAL HAVE A DEADLINE?

As you are probably aware, you must accomplish your goals with a target schedule. You must carry out a series of activities and tasks within the given time frame.

Making your goal time-based helps you create and work on your plan according to a targeted deadline.
Without setting a specific timeline, you would not know when you can complete your plan - as you do not create a sense of urgency.
You are probably familiar with this expression, "I don't have the time..." Most people could relate to not having the time to do certain things. If that is the case, you

could conclude that the person does not seem to want to prioritize the need to do it. Do you see any point of urgency there?

How do you expect a person to accomplish a goal when there is no time to do the necessary tasks?

Did you get the point?

* * *

WHAT ARE YOU SAVING FOR?

Creating a healthy savings mix would require that you look at your goals and priorities.

Then, you will have to decide which of these goals you would put in your list of short-term goals, medium-term goals, and long-term goals.

Let us explore what some of your goals might be by considering the following possibilities.

- *Paying Yourself First (Or Your Monthly Savings)*
- *Semi-Annual Budget (6 months of Projected Expenses)*
- *Emergency Savings (Rainy-day Savings)*
- *Down Payment (For Home Purchase)*
- *Mortgage (Covering 3-6 Months Payments)*
- *Car Purchase*
- *College (Or Education Fund)*
- *Retirement Savings*

Is there anything in particular that you need to prioritize?

Can you think and identify which of your goals would be your short-term goals, medium-term goals, and long-term goals? If there's anything in particular that you need to prioritize (but has not been mentioned), feel free to include it.

There might be some more things that you could, perhaps, consider or include in your list. However, it is much better to avoid getting overwhelmed with so many goals. It is best to plan one goal at a given time. Make things simple, especially if you are a beginner. You will be able to go through the process a lot easier.

How much money should you start to save?

Of course, people would have different answers to this question. Some people find it necessary to save at least an amount that equates to six (6) months of expenses.

For example, if you estimate that your monthly personal expenses would be one-thousand dollars ($1000.00) and you are saving for six (6) months, then your goal would be to achieve the amount of six thousand dollars ($6000.00).

How do you think you could achieve your savings goals? What would be your strategies?

SEVEN

CREATING YOUR INVESTMENT MIX AS A BEGINNING INVESTOR

Creating Your Investment Mix
As a Beginning Investor

CHAPTER SEVEN

- Where to Put Your Money
- A Whole New Journey
- Savings Account
- Investment Mix and Diversification
- Should You Do Stock Investing
- Mutual Funds
- Exchange Traded Funds
- Robo-advisor
- Conclusion

WHERE TO PUT YOUR MONEY

Coming up with your investing strategies is never simple and easy.

There's the thought about where you should put your hard-earned money - so that you could make it work for you.

Some people might have some ideas.

Some could ask, "How much should I put in each part of my investment mix?"

But some people do not seem to have any clue at all - "How and where should I invest my money wisely?"

A WHOLE NEW JOURNEY

If you look at it, somehow, learning about investing could be a whole new journey.

You might even wonder, "Who could find the time to work on this personal finance topic?"

Not to mention the fact that - you may not even have enough money to work on at this point.

So how could you even entertain the idea of setting aside some money for investments, right?

But wait, how come others could do it?

You might be a beginner in this concept (of investing and saving money), but this could be a good point with which you can start.

At first, you will find the subject to be somewhat complicated.

The concept of money alone could be already overwhelming. How much more when we touch on the idea of investing? You have perhaps heard about the words: volatility and risks. If you must know, these words are often associated with investments.

The moment you begin investing your money through various forms, you would then become more familiar with some sorts of risks.

Hence, you might even ask and convince yourself at this point, "Why not just leave my money in the bank? It will earn an interest anyway, right? And it is easier."

SAVINGS ACCOUNT

Opening a savings account is a safe means to save money especially if, you have not navigated the many other forms of investments.

At least, there's that goal on your part to get started with something. That's a real good start.

When you decide to open and maintain a savings account, make sure that your money is earning the highest interest rate your bank could offer - compared to other financial products.

You could browse and conduct a comparison of rates online.

You could search and find available financial products and their corresponding rates.

Which bank could offer a better return?

If you are not satisfied, you are better off looking at other options.

INVESTMENT MIX AND DIVERSIFICATION

If you prefer to grow your money in many other ways, there are several options you could consider to create your investment mix.

There are some questions that you need to ask yourself first.

How much longer time horizon do I have?

Am I ready to consider a much higher return on investment despite the risks involved (in investing my money)?

Some people look at investing their money in a combination of several investment forms.

Mutual Funds;
ETFs;
High-Yield Bonds;
Government Bonds;
Short-Term Bonds;
Real Estate;
Emerging Markets;
Dividend Stocks;
US Stocks;
Canadian Stocks; and
Foreign Stocks.

Given these technical, financial investment terms, it is understandable that as a beginner, you may be confused.

You might ask, "How much should I put in (each part of) the investment mix?"

Have you heard of the investment strategy using diversification?

The concept of diversification is about putting your money across plenty of different baskets.

At this point, you might want to consider the idea of diversification.

> The concept of diversification is about putting your money across plenty of different baskets.

With diversification, you have a well-balanced approach. And as a result, you could earn a better return on your investment in the long run. You would also be able to minimize risks.

SHOULD YOU DO STOCK INVESTING

If you are a beginner and you have not traded stocks ever in your adult life, your best route is to learn as much as you can about the 'ins and outs' of stock investing, at the earliest opportunity, prior to jumping into the stock trading field.

Do you know when and why you should buy or sell a particular stock?

Do you like to read and monitor stock market news? How about the global and economic performance?

What industry are you familiar with? How well do you know the company you would invest in as a shareholder?

What is your thought about risks? Do you know your risk level?

What kind of investor are you? Conservative? Growth seeker?

Would you rather have a Balanced portfolio?

Stock investing can be risky.

If you would like to pursue trading and investing in stocks (buying or selling of shares), make sure you are equipped with proper knowledge.

How about pursuing another avenue to get into investing in stocks?

If you are not ready yet to directly put money in stocks, it is best that you become familiar with some investment instruments. You might want to learn the concepts about mutual funds, exchange-traded funds (or ETFs), and Robo-advisors.

MUTUAL FUNDS

Many investors have put money in mutual funds for many years as their investment vehicle.

In fact, according to the website of The Investment Funds Institute of Canada 'Stats and Facts' (https://www.ific.ca), mutual funds make up about thirty-one percent (31%) of Canadians' financial wealth.

So what is a mutual fund?

A mutual fund is an investment fund available to investors, which is managed professionally by fund managers. Orders on mutual funds are executed after the market closes, and can be placed with the help of a mutual fund advisor or brokerage.

Mutual funds put together money from many investors and invest the pooled funds in securities, such as stocks, bonds and other assets. Each investing individual or entity would then own shares or fund units.

For beginners, purchasing mutual funds can be a bit overwhelming. New investors, depending on their investment experience, may encounter many unfamiliar terms that may be difficult to understand.

Many financial companies and banks offer certain mutual funds.

If you are not familiar with this kind of fund investment, do not hesitate to research further. Read the information and prospectus provided to you.

You could also look at other sources online. You should try to learn more about the mutual fund in which you specifically plan to invest.

Banks and financial companies have advisors that can help you get started.

However, you should only invest (or put money) in financial investments that you clearly understand.

There are also certified financial planners that specialize in this area. And you could consult with them. Some financial planners may charge a fee. There are investment consultants who could get paid in the form of a commission or management fees. The amount or rate of which would depend on the fund that you select.

EXCHANGE TRADED FUNDS (ETF)

Then, here comes the concept of Exchange Traded Funds (ETFs). Investing in ETFs has become popular in recent years.

Similar to a mutual fund, an exchange traded fund (ETF) can have a mix of securities or stocks - tracking a stock index or stock market index. The ETF can also invest in a mix of industries or invest using a variety of strategies.

ETF can be purchased or sold throughout the day on stock exchanges, such as The Toronto Stock Exchange (TSX), The New York Stock Exchange (NYSE), and other stock exchanges, where the ETF can be traded.

Investing in ETFs makes a lot of sense, given the idea of diversification, risk-management, and the simple investment approach. One can invest in ETFs regularly, depending on how much you can set aside on a specific schedule. Some brokerages can even offer free trading fees on ETFs.

ROBO-ADVISOR

Have you ever heard of robo-advisor?

A robo-advisor is available through a digital platform that provides an auto-pilot investing service to investors.

Such a digital platform would enable the process. One would think a wealth manager is performing the task. But, in essence, the software is the one that analyzes your profile as an investor.

To get started, you usually have to answer a set of questions. That should help assess your level of risk in which you could be comfortable. Also, that should help analyze where to put your money across investments and make adjustments when necessary (or depending on the market situation).

Investing in this manner could help you build an investment mix, considering the level of risks you're comfortable with, whether you're looking at a balanced investment fund, conservative investment fund, or growth fund.

CONCLUSION

By now, you must know that your savings goals and investing strategies would all depend on the totality of your financial outlook.

The outcome or success of your financial undertakings would depend on how you prepare and execute your financial plan.

Get to know more of yourself, how you feel about your circumstances, how you think about the influences around you, and how you face and tackle the financial challenges that come your way.

It pays to gain knowledge and apply approaches that you believe will work for you.

Ultimately, the answer lies in your hands. Know where you are. Know your goals. Know where you're going. Find a way to get there.

ABOUT THE AUTHOR

Sheila Atienza is a Canadian author and content creator who writes about personal finance, real estate, small business and marketing. Sheila has had over a decade of experience in the real estate industry. She now pursues her passion for digital media, research, content writing, and publishing projects.

Some of her published works/books are available in:

University of Toronto Thomas Fisher Library; McGill University; Dalhousie University DAL Killam Library; Brown University; Library and Archives nationales du Québec; Canada Mortgage Housing Corporation; Medicine Hat College; Loyalist College; and other libraries across Canada and the U.S.A.

She is the author of the books: "Micro Enterprise Marketing: How to Start, Promote and Grow Your Micro Business in the Digital Age," "Tweets for Your Thoughts," "How to Prepare to Own a Home in Canada," and "Canadian Home Financing Simplified."

Sheila is also a marketing professional and digital media consultant based in B.C., Canada.